INSPECTOR THACKERAY *calls*

Kenneth James and Lloyd Mullen

Illustrations by Mark Oldroyd

Addison Wesley Longman Limited
Edinburgh Gate, Harlow,
Essex CM20 2JE, England
and Associated Companies throughout the world

© Longman Group Limited 1974
© Addison Wesley Longman Limited 1997

All rights reserved; no part of this publication may be reproduced, stored in a retrieval system, or transmitted in any form or by any means, electronic, mechanical, photocopying, recording, or otherwise, without the prior written permission of the Publishers.

First published 1974 in Longman Structural Readers
This edition first published 1997 in Longman Originals
Second impression 1997

Illustrations by Mark Oldroyd

Set in 10.5/12pt Melior

Printed in China
EPC/02

ISBN 0 582 27397 8

Contents

The train robbers   5

Death at Hilltop Cottage   23

The driver didn't stop   37

The game of chess   48

Reading activities   62

BEXLEY LIBRARY SERVICE			
LOC CL	CL No. 428.6 JAM		
PRICE 2.70	ACC 20.10.99		GT
COLL CODE NEADLIT	ITEM LOAN TYPE JUB	
KEYER		LANG	CH	PR

25/10

The train robbers

CHARACTERS

INSPECTOR THACKERAY
SERGEANT SILVER
NEWSREADER
RADIO REPORTER
GUARD
POLICE OFFICER
PC ROBSON

Scene 1

(News room. BBC Radio Four.)

NEWSREADER This is the BBC Radio News, at one o'clock… Stories are still reaching us about the big train robbery near Manchester. Our reporter in Manchester is Colin Walker. He has just sent us this report.

REPORTER This is Colin Walker in Piccadilly Station, Manchester. The police have now arrived here in large numbers. They are using the waiting-room as a police station. I'm standing outside there now. Inside the police are very busy. Telephones are ringing and officers have already started to type out reports. A sergeant is putting a large railway map on the wall. And the driver of the train is answering questions in the far corner… Of course, the big question is – how much money is missing? Well, we don't know that yet. Ah – here's Inspector Thackeray. He's in charge of the case… Excuse me. Excuse me, Inspector. Colin Walker, BBC.

THACKERAY I'm sorry, Mr Walker. I'm very busy at the moment. Later perhaps.

REPORTER Just a few questions, sir, before you go in. They'll only take a minute.

THACKERAY All right, then. One minute.

REPORTER How much money was there on the train?

THACKERAY Two million pounds.

REPORTER Two million! Why did it have to go by train to Manchester?

THACKERAY The Bank of England's orders. They wanted to print some new notes. So first they had to burn the old ones.

REPORTER And who took the money?

THACKERAY We think there were three thieves.

REPORTER Three? Do you know their names yet?

THACKERAY No.

REPORTER What have you found out about them?

THACKERAY I'm sorry. I can't answer that question. I must go now.

REPORTER Inspector…

THACKERAY Excuse me. *(He goes.)*

REPORTER Well, that's the latest news. There were three thieves. And they took two million pounds. This is Colin Walker, Piccadilly Station, Manchester.

Scene 2

(The station waiting-room.)

THACKERAY Ah, Sergeant Silver. You've put up the railway map. Good.

SILVER Ah, there you are, sir. We were waiting for you. Look at this. I think it's important.

THACKERAY Mm. A cigar-end. What kind is it?

SILVER I don't know, sir. There's no name on it.

THACKERAY Of course there isn't. But a detective ought to be able to name any cigar.

SILVER How?

THACKERAY By its smell.

SILVER Sorry, sir. I don't smoke.

THACKERAY Didn't they teach you about these things at the police college?

SILVER   No, sir. There were a few classes on drugs, though.

THACKERAY   Drugs. Mm. Give it to me, then. *(He smells the cigar.)* Well this is a Havana, lad. Yes – a good Havana. One of these costs about eight pounds.

SILVER   Eight pounds for a cigar? That's a lot.

THACKERAY   Where did you find it?

SILVER   On the floor of the guard's van.

THACKERAY   The guard's van. We must go back to the train, then. Have the fingerprint men finished there yet?

SILVER   Yes. And the guard feels better now. He says he can answer some questions.

THACKERAY   Good. Where is he?

SILVER   We took him back to the guard's van. He's waiting there for you.

THACKERAY   Alone?

SILVER   No, sir. There's a police constable with him.

THACKERAY   All right. Where is this van now?

SILVER   At the end of the train. At the far end of the station.

OFFICER   Inspector Bates is on the telephone for you, sir.

THACKERAY   Not now. Tell him I've left. I'm going to the guard's van.

Scene 3

(Outside the guard's van. PC Robson is standing in front of the door.)

SILVER Here's the van, sir. And this is Police Constable Robson.

THACKERAY Robson.

ROBSON Sir.

THACKERAY Have the fingerprint men gone?

ROBSON Yes, sir.

SILVER What did they find?

ROBSON Not much. The thieves were wearing gloves.

THACKERAY Were they?

ROBSON Yes, sir.

THACKERAY The guard's inside, is he?

ROBSON Yes, sir.

THACKERAY Well, we won't need you now, Constable. You must be tired.
If you go back to the waiting-room you can get a cup of tea.

ROBSON Right, sir. Thank you.

THACKERAY Right, then. Now we'll hear the guard's story.

SILVER Allow me, sir. This door's heavy.

THACKERAY I'll open it, lad. I'm not an old man yet...
You're right, you know. It *is* heavy.

SILVER I told you it was.

Scene 4

(The Inspector and Sergeant Silver go into the guard's van. There are mail bags and letters on the floor. The guard is sitting on a stool in the corner.)

GUARD Who are you?

SILVER This is Inspector Thackeray.

THACKERAY Perhaps I can ask a few questions.

GUARD Oh. Yes.

THACKERAY Hey – you're still very white. Are you all right?

GUARD Oh yes, sir. I'm better now.

THACKERAY A lot of noise here, isn't there?

GUARD I'll shut the door, sir.

THACKERAY No, that's all right. My sergeant will do it. He's younger than us.

SILVER *(Closing the door)* And stronger, sir.

THACKERAY Mm. Yes. Perhaps. Now, first, what's your name?

GUARD Jones. Arthur Jones.

THACKERAY Put that in your notebook, will you Sergeant? I want you to make notes of this conversation.

SILVER Yes, sir. 'Arthur Jones.'

THACKERAY I think I'll smoke my pipe. If you'll allow me, Mr Jones?

GUARD Oh yes.

THACKERAY I can never find my matches. Do you have any matches, Mr Jones?

GUARD No, sir. I don't smoke.

SILVER They're in your top right-hand pocket, sir. You always put them there.

THACKERAY Ah yes. Thank you, Silver. Now Mr Jones. Just tell me your story. Nice and slowly.

GUARD Well now – er – yes. I was counting the mail bags...

THACKERAY Where?

GUARD Over here, sir, in this corner.

SILVER And what time was that?

GUARD Almost twelve o'clock.

SILVER Twelve o'clock. Good. Don't stop.

GUARD Well, I was counting the mail bags. And there was a knock at the door.

THACKERAY This door, at the end of the van?

GUARD Yes, sir. That one. You came in through it.

THACKERAY Ah yes. These doors are heavy, aren't they?

GUARD Yes. They're very thick and very strong. They have to be, on a train.

THACKERAY How many times did they knock?

GUARD Twice.

THACKERAY You're certain?

GUARD Yes, I'm certain.

SILVER What happened then?

GUARD Well – I opened the door.

SILVER You were guarding two million pounds? And you opened the door – against your orders?

GUARD Yes, against my orders. I was wrong.

THACKERAY But – why? Why did you open it?

GUARD The ticket inspector knocks sometimes. I thought it was him.

SILVER The ticket inspector?

GUARD Yes. These are long journeys, you know. He sometimes brings me a cup of tea.

THACKERAY A cup of tea? Huh! All right. What happened then?

GUARD Three men came in. They pushed me back into the van.

THACKERAY Three men. Can you remember them?

GUARD Not very well, really. It happened so quickly.

THACKERAY Try.

GUARD Well – er, yes, I know. Two were tall. And one was quite short.

SILVER Can you remember their faces?

THACKERAY Yes, what about their faces?

GUARD I couldn't see them. They had stockings over their heads.

SILVER *(Writing)* 'Stockings...' What about their clothes? Their shoes?

GUARD Black. Yes – black coats and shoes. But not the short man. He was wearing a grey coat. Yes, that's right, a grey one.

THACKERAY What about their hands?

GUARD They wore gloves.

THACKERAY Well – what did they do to you?

GUARD They pushed me into this corner.

THACKERAY That's a cut on your face, Mr Jones. Did they do that?

GUARD Oh yes. They did.

SILVER With a knife?

GUARD No. They didn't have knives.

THACKERAY How did it happen then?

GUARD One of them was wearing a ring.

THACKERAY Was he? What kind of ring?

GUARD I'm sorry. I can't remember very well.

SILVER It cut you. You must remember it.

GUARD No, sorry. Oh yes – there was one thing. It was gold.

SILVER You're certain?

GUARD Well, no, I'm not certain. But it was yellow.

THACKERAY All right. And then?

GUARD Well, then they tied me to this chair here.

THACKERAY Yes?

GUARD *(He takes a handkerchief out of his pocket.)* Then they tied this handkerchief over my eyes.

THACKERAY Oh, can I have a look at it? *(He takes the handkerchief and examines it.)* Thank you. Mm. Blue and white – yes, it cost quite a lot. We'll keep this handkerchief, Mr Jones.

SILVER I'll ask the laboratory for a report on it, sir.

THACKERAY Yes. Thank you, Sergeant. You take it. *(He gives the handkerchief to Sergeant Silver.)* Now, Mr Jones. These three men. What did they say?

GUARD I don't know. I couldn't hear them.

THACKERAY You couldn't hear them. Why was that?

GUARD The train was going very fast. It was making a lot of noise.

THACKERAY Yes, they do, don't they? But tell me – when did these men leave the train?

GUARD I don't really know.

THACKERAY Try to remember. Your answer can help us.

GUARD Oh yes. Ten minutes later. We stopped at some signals. The train was quiet for a moment. I thought I heard the outside door open. Perhaps they jumped out then.

SILVER *(Writing)* 'Stopped at signals.' There's that railway map in the waiting-room, sir. That shows the signals.

THACKERAY Yes it does. I forgot that. We'll have a look at it later.

GUARD Can I go now, Inspector? I'm still not very well.

THACKERAY In a minute. I've just one last question.

GUARD What's that?

THACKERAY You don't smoke, do you?

GUARD No, I've told you that.

THACKERAY Well, one of my policemen found this cigar-end.

GUARD Where?

THACKERAY In this van. On the floor here.

GUARD Well, I didn't smoke it.

SILVER Who did?

GUARD I don't know. Oh yes I do – I remember now. The short man. He smoked it.

THACKERAY Are you quite certain?

GUARD Yes. The short one. He never took it out of his mouth.

SILVER Never?

GUARD Well, not while I could see him.

THE TRAIN ROBBERS

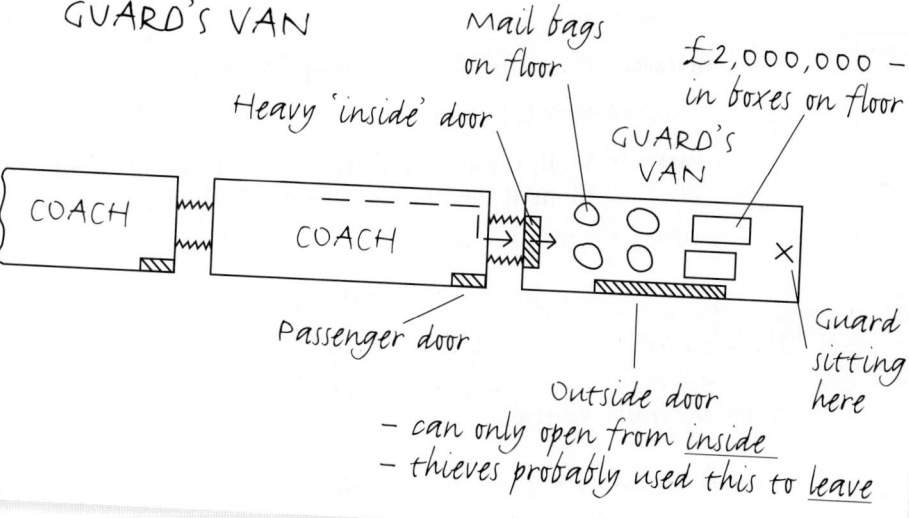

(Constable Robson enters.)

ROBSON Excuse me, sir.

THACKERAY What is it, Constable?

ROBSON Telephone for you, sir.

THACKERAY What's it about?

ROBSON A man from the BBC.

THACKERAY I've already talked to him.

ROBSON   He was from the radio, sir. This man's from television. It's for the six o'clock news.

SILVER   But we haven't caught the thieves yet.

THACKERAY   Perhaps. Perhaps not.

SILVER   Have we?

THACKERAY   I'll see him at the police station in half an hour, Constable.

ROBSON   Very well, sir. I'll tell him.

THACKERAY   Come on, Silver. You too, Mr Jones.

GUARD   Me? Why me?

THACKERAY   Well, three reasons really. We can talk about them at the police station. Shall we go?

THIEVES

Description from guard –

3 men: 2 tall, 1 short
   stockings over their faces
   gloves – no fingerprints!!
   tall men – black coats and shoes
   short man – grey coat

Voices? Couldn't hear v. well. Train made a lot of noise.

GUARD

Name – JONES, Arthur
Age – late thirties
Description – black hair, brown eyes, about 1.8 metres
 thin, not v. strong
 cut on face (says from gold/yellow ring worn by one thief) and torn clothes
 non-smoker (says short thief smoked cigar)

GUARD'S STORY

1. About 12 noon – counting mail bags
2. Two knocks on inside door – guard opened it
3. Thieves entered (not ticket inspector with tea!)
4. Tied him up, handkerchief round eyes
5. Train stopped at signals. (Thieves left?) – about 12.10
6. Arrived Manchester, ticket inspector came – called police

NB Send cigar & handkerchief to laboratory for report.

Scene 5

Inspector Thackeray explains

(Manchester Central Police Station. The office of Inspector Thackeray and Sergeant Silver.)

THACKERAY Come into the office and we'll talk.

SILVER I'll get a chair for Mr Jones.

THACKERAY Yes. Good.

SILVER Oh, and that flower-pot, sir. Do you really want it on your desk?

THACKERAY Oh yes. I was going to water my flowers this morning, wasn't I? Yes. You move it please, Silver. I need to put my papers here now.

SILVER Right, sir. I'll put it back in the window.

GUARD Flowers in a policeman's office! You're a strange one, Inspector.

THACKERAY You must be a city man, Mr Jones.

GUARD Yes, I am. I come from London.

SILVER The Inspector comes from the country.

THACKERAY And these roses help me to remember it.

SILVER There you are, Mr Jones. There's your chair.

GUARD Thank you.

THACKERAY That's better, isn't it?

GUARD Yes. Well, Inspector. I've told you my story. What do you want now?

THACKERAY The answer to one last question.

GUARD What's that?

THACKERAY Where have you put the money?

GUARD Me? I didn't take it.

THACKERAY If you tell us now, perhaps you won't go to prison later.

GUARD But why me? Why don't you look for those three men?

THACKERAY Oh yes. The three men. Where are they, Mr Jones?

GUARD I don't know, do I? Look, Inspector. They hit me, and they tied me up. One of them even cut my face.

SILVER Oh yes. The one with the ring.

GUARD That's right.

THACKERAY But they were all wearing gloves, weren't they?

GUARD Er – yes... that's right.

THACKERAY But you saw a ring.

GUARD Er – no, I didn't *see* it. I *felt* it.

THACKERAY You only felt it?

GUARD Yes. When he hit my face.

THACKERAY Sergeant.

SILVER Sir?

THACKERAY Your notebook, please.

SILVER Oh. Yes. Of course.

THACKERAY Sergeant Silver wrote down the conversation in his notebook. Perhaps you remember. What did Mr Jones say about the ring, Sergeant?

SILVER I have the words here. He said, "It was gold." And later, "It was yellow."

GUARD All right. I made a mistake.

THACKERAY Oh, not just one, Mr Jones. Not just one. You don't smoke, do you?

GUARD No. I told you before.

THACKERAY Then who smoked that cigar?

GUARD One of the thieves. I explained that before.

THACKERAY Did you see him?

GUARD Yes. I told you.

THACKERAY Notebook, Sergeant?

SILVER Mr Jones said, "He never took it out of his mouth."

THACKERAY Very strange.

GUARD No, it isn't. A lot of people smoke like that.

THACKERAY And do they wear stockings over their faces? How do they smoke at the same time? What's the answer, Mr Jones?

GUARD I don't know.

THACKERAY Now. These three men. They're your friends, aren't they? Where have they put the money?

GUARD I don't know.

THACKERAY All right then. What did they say in the guard's van?

GUARD I couldn't hear them. I told you. The train made too much noise.

THACKERAY But you opened the door. The door of the guard's van.

GUARD Yes. I heard a knock.

SILVER Two knocks. They knocked twice, you said.

GUARD All right, two knocks.

THACKERAY But isn't that strange, Mr Jones? You could hear two knocks on that door. A thick, heavy door like that. But you couldn't hear a word from the thieves.

SILVER And they were standing next to you.

THACKERAY No, I'm sorry, Mr Jones. It's not a very good story, is it?

(There is a knock at the door.)

THACKERAY Come in.

ROBSON Excuse me, sir. The man from television is ready.

THACKERAY I'm coming. Take Mr Jones downstairs, Constable. *(The Inspector turns to Mr Jones.)* Sergeant Silver will come down in a few minutes, Mr Jones. This time you'll tell the true story. All right, Constable. Take him down now.

ROBSON This way, Mr Jones.

(Mr Jones and the constable leave.)

THACKERAY I don't like this television interview, Silver.

SILVER Don't you, sir?

THACKERAY No. I like to ask the questions, not answer them.

SILVER I've noticed that, sir.

THACKERAY And who wants to see *me* on television? I'm a policeman – not a pop-star.

SILVER That's certainly very true, sir. But TV interviews are quite easy really.

THACKERAY How do you know?

SILVER I've done a few.

THACKERAY Have you? Where?

SILVER At the police college. They trained us to answer questions in front of a camera. They said it was very important. You know, public relations work. *(Pause)* They didn't have a class on cigars though, sir.

THACKERAY Don't be funny, Silver.

SILVER Sorry, sir.

THACKERAY And before you go down and see Jones –

SILVER Yes, sir?

THACKERAY Water those roses. I won't have time today.

Death at Hilltop Cottage

CHARACTERS

INSPECTOR THACKERAY
SERGEANT SILVER
DOCTOR JOHNSON
MRS PARKER

Scene 1

(It is a hot summer's day in Woodley, a small village outside Manchester. Inspector Thackeray and Sergeant Silver are watching a cricket match.)

THACKERAY I was born here, you know. It's a beautiful place isn't it?

SILVER Yes sir. If you like the country…

THACKERAY *(Thackeray's mobile phone rings.)* Thackeray here… What? Yes, I'm in Woodley village, watching the cricket… What? A death at Hilltop Cottage! No, our car's parked a mile away – we'll walk.

SILVER It's probably an accident, sir. There are very few crimes in these small villages.

(Five minutes later, the two policemen are near the top of the hill. A man is working in the garden of a cottage in front of them.)

THACKERAY Come on, lad. What's the matter with you?

SILVER It's hot and you're walking too fast.

THACKERAY Oh, Silver. Five minutes' walk up a hill, and you're tired already. When I was your age…

SILVER Is this the cottage, sir?

THACKERAY I don't know. There's a man in the garden. Excuse me.

JOHNSON Hello there.

THACKERAY Is this Hilltop Cottage?

JOHNSON No. That's the next one. Can I help you?

SILVER Does Mrs Parker live there?

JOHNSON Yes, she does.

SILVER Is she in now?

JOHNSON Well, she was there at lunchtime.

THACKERAY Oh, was she?
JOHNSON Yes, they came up here from the village together.
THACKERAY They?
JOHNSON Mr and Mrs Parker. But who are you?
THACKERAY And then they went into the house?
JOHNSON That's right. But she came here later, and made a telephone call.
SILVER A telephone call?
JOHNSON Yes. It was very strange. She was crying. I've never seen her like that before.
SILVER Haven't they got a phone?
JOHNSON No. They're new here. They're waiting for a new phone line. You're friends are you?
THACKERAY Does she use your phone a lot?
JOHNSON No. Usually they use the phone at the shop.
SILVER Which shop is that?
JOHNSON Smith's. You know. At the bottom of the hill. Next to the cricket ground.
THACKERAY And why did she come to *you* this time?
JOHNSON Well, it was lunchtime. The shop was closed. But why –
SILVER What time does it close for lunch?
JOHNSON From 12.30 to 1.30. I say, you're not the police are you?
THACKERAY Who did she phone? Do you know?
JOHNSON No, I didn't hear. I was cutting wood at the back. But why are you asking so many questions?
THACKERAY Thank you very much. You've been most helpful.

SILVER   Yes, sir. You know, you've a nice garden there, sir.

THACKERAY   You don't know a thing about gardens, Silver. Come on. *(He starts to walk up the hill again.)*

SILVER   Those are lovely flowers.

THACKERAY   Be quick, Silver.

JOHNSON   Hey! *Are* you the police?

THACKERAY   Silver.

SILVER   Coming, sir.

Scene 2

(Inspector Thackeray and Sergeant Silver have reached the front door of the next cottage.)

SILVER   This is really Hilltop Cottage, is it?

THACKERAY   *(Knocking at the door)* Use your eyes, lad. The name's over the door.

SILVER   Oh yes.

THACKERAY   A better garden, this one.

MRS PARKER   *(Opening the door)* Are you the police?

THACKERAY   Yes. My name is…

MRS PARKER   Oh, thank God you've come. It's my husband. My husband…

THACKERAY   Now wait a minute. First, are you Mrs Parker?

MRS PARKER   Yes, I am.

THACKERAY   Well, I'm Inspector Thackeray, and this is Sergeant Silver.

MRS PARKER   Yes, yes. Come in, please.

(The two policemen go into the front room.)

THACKERAY Now then. What's the trouble?

MRS PARKER It's my husband. He's killed himself.

SILVER Suicide? Are you certain?

MRS PARKER Yes, certain. It was suicide. I know it was.

THACKERAY Has a doctor seen him yet?

MRS PARKER No, not yet.

THACKERAY Well then – I'm sorry – but I'll have to see the body, Mrs Parker. Have you got your notebook ready, Sergeant?

SILVER Ready.

MRS PARKER He's in the room at the back. Come this way, will you?

Scene 3

(The back room. The body is on the floor in the middle of the room. A desk with some papers on it stands in one corner. The large window looks on to a beautiful garden at the back.)

MRS PARKER There he is, Inspector.

THACKERAY Thank you. Silver, take Mrs Parker to that chair there.

SILVER Yes, sir. Sit down here, Mrs Parker. Next to the window. You can look at the garden from here.

MRS PARKER Thank you, Sergeant.

THACKERAY *(Quietly)* Now lad. Here's the body. How did it happen?

SILVER He shot himself. Straight through the head. And with this gun.

THACKERAY No, don't touch it. Leave it in his hand.

SILVER His finger is still on the trigger.

THACKERAY He died when he pulled it.

SILVER There was no pain, then.

MRS PARKER *(Loudly)* What do you know about pain?

SILVER Sorry!

THACKERAY Mrs Parker, I shall have to ask you some questions now. Is that all right?

MRS PARKER Yes, Inspector.

THACKERAY When did you see your husband last?

MRS PARKER Before he killed himself?

THACKERAY Yes. Alive.

MRS PARKER Alive – yes – it was outside the shop. In the village.

SILVER What time was that?

MRS PARKER Oh, a quarter past twelve. He left me and came up here.

THACKERAY Why? Did he say?

MRS PARKER There was a letter. Yes, he suddenly remembered an important letter. About some business, he said. He had to write it quickly.

THACKERAY Did he use his car?

MRS PARKER No. It's gone to the garage today. It needs a service.

THACKERAY And when did it happen? When did he kill himself? Have you any idea?

MRS PARKER Yes. Between quarter to one and one o'clock.

THACKERAY How do you know that, Mrs Parker?

MRS PARKER Well, he left the village at a quarter past twelve. And he usually walked up here in half an hour.

SILVER So he got here at quarter to one?

MRS PARKER Yes, and I arrived at one o'clock.

THACKERAY Why didn't you come up here with him?

MRS PARKER I had to buy some things in the shop. I came up later.

THACKERAY When you found your husband, what did you do?

MRS PARKER Well, I just sat down. I couldn't think for a minute. It was terrible. Terrible.

SILVER Then you telephoned?

MRS PARKER Yes. From Hillside House.

SILVER Where?

MRS PARKER Hillside House. You know. Dr Johnson's. It's the next house down the hill.

SILVER Oh, he's a doctor, is he? Oh yes. We met him.

THACKERAY All right. Now, about the gun.

MRS PARKER I've never seen it before.

THACKERAY Is it your husband's?

MRS PARKER I'm not certain. Perhaps it is.

THACKERAY I want you to be brave now. I'm going to ask you a question. Perhaps a painful question. Tell me, Mrs Parker. Why did he kill himself?

MRS PARKER I don't know.

THACKERAY No idea?

MRS PARKER He was losing a lot of money in his business.

THACKERAY How much has he lost?

MRS PARKER Oh, several thousand pounds.

SILVER Excuse me, sir. There's a letter on the table here. Perhaps that will explain.

THACKERAY Well done, Sergeant. Give it to me, please.

SILVER Yes sir. Here you are.

THACKERAY Yes. It's to the bank.

MRS PARKER What does it say?

THACKERAY *(Reading)* "Dear Sir. Thank you very much for the ten thousand pounds. I can continue my business now. And I will –"

MRS PARKER Is that all?

THACKERAY It finishes there.

SILVER What? In the middle of a sentence?

THACKERAY Yes. Strange. He had good news from the bank. Not bad news.

MRS PARKER Do you think I'm wrong then? Perhaps he didn't want to kill himself.

SILVER Yes, sir. Perhaps it was an accident.

THACKERAY An accident? But how?

MRS PARKER Well, I don't know. Perhaps he took the gun out of his room upstairs. And he was going to clean it.

SILVER And knocked it? Or touched the trigger?

MRS PARKER Yes. And it killed him.

THACKERAY Tell me just one thing, Mrs Parker. And please think carefully. When you left the shop, what time was it?

MRS PARKER Five to one.

THACKERAY Certain?

MRS PARKER Oh yes. I remember. I looked at the church clock just then.

SILVER Well, what do you think, sir?

THACKERAY I don't think, Silver. I *know*. I'm sorry, Mrs Parker. But this wasn't an accident. And it wasn't suicide.

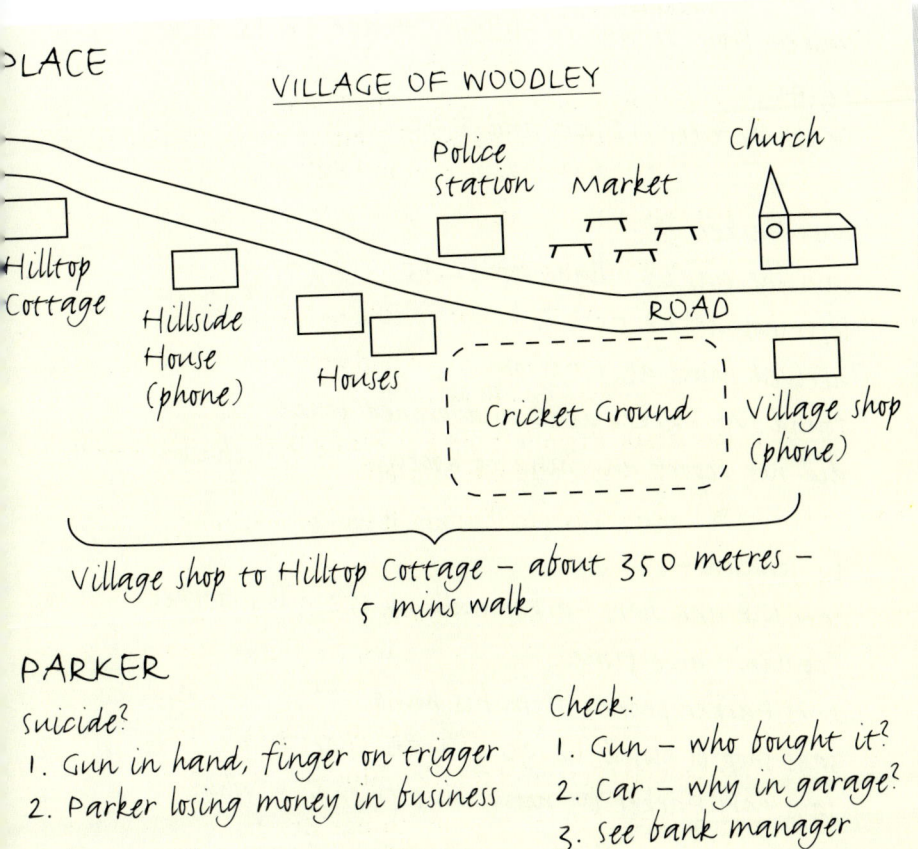

TIME/MOVEMENTS

Mr Parker –
remembered important letter (when in village)
walked from village to Hilltop Cottage 12.15 to 12.45.
Death between 12.45 and 1.00

Mrs Parker –
says she was in village at 12.15
left shop at 12.55
arrived home at 1.00 pm
found Mr Parker dead and phoned police
did not report anything to doctor – or Dr Johnson

Dr Johnson –
saw Mr and Mrs Parker walk up the hill together (couldn't give time)
Mrs Parker phoned from his house
says shop is closed 12.30 – 1.30 (Mrs P?)
says Mrs Parker is "not a close friend" – why?

Scene 4

Inspector Thackeray explains

(In the front room again.)

MRS PARKER I think I need a rest. Can I make some tea for you?

SILVER That's very kind —

THACKERAY No, thank you. I still need some answers, Mrs Parker.

MRS PARKER Oh yes. Of course.

THACKERAY Now think. Did you walk up the hill alone?

MRS PARKER Yes.

THACKERAY But Doctor Johnson saw you with your husband.

MRS PARKER Did he say that?

THACKERAY He did. You don't like him, do you?

MRS PARKER Did he say that, too?

THACKERAY No. I'm saying that. *(Pause)* You know, I don't understand you, Mrs Parker.

MRS PARKER Oh?

THACKERAY Yes. You come back and find your husband on the floor. A gun beside him. And there's a doctor in the next house. But you don't run for help.

MRS PARKER He was already dead.

THACKERAY Was he?

SILVER But surely only a doctor can say that?

THACKERAY And you didn't even ask him.

MRS PARKER He was dead, I tell you. The gun killed him.

THACKERAY That gun, Mrs Parker. Where did it come from?

MRS PARKER I never saw it before this afternoon.

SILVER Yes, you said that before.

THACKERAY But then you changed your story.

MRS PARKER Changed it?

THACKERAY Your notebook, Sergeant.

SILVER Er – yes – you're quite right, sir. She did change her story. You said – and these are your own words, Mrs Parker – "Perhaps he took the gun out of his room upstairs."

THACKERAY "Out of his room upstairs." How did you know it was there?

MRS PARKER Well – I just thought it came from there. Oh, please stop these questions. I'm so tired. I've told you my story.

THACKERAY Oh, but you haven't. There's the walk up the hill. Tell me about that, Mrs Parker.

MRS PARKER The walk up the hill! What about it?

THACKERAY Well now. I'm not a young man, Mrs Parker. And I walked up this hill in five minutes. You and your husband are young people. You said you only took five minutes yourself, Mrs Parker.

MRS PARKER Did I?

THACKERAY Notebook, Sergeant?

SILVER Correct. Left the shop at five to one. Reached here at one o'clock. Five minutes.

THACKERAY But your husband usually took half an hour. You told us that too.

MRS PARKER Yes.

THACKERAY Half an hour. Why?

MRS PARKER He walked slowly.

THACKERAY Why?

MRS PARKER He just liked to.

THACKERAY He left you in the village. Remember? That was your story.

MRS PARKER It's true. He suddenly remembered a letter.

THACKERAY Oh yes, the letter. An important letter. And he had to write it quickly. Quickly, Mrs Parker. So why half an hour? Was he ill, Mrs Parker?

MRS PARKER Why do you think that?

THACKERAY I'll tell you why. A strange thing happened when I was talking to my Sergeant before. You shouted at him. When was it, Sergeant?

SILVER We were looking at the body, I think, sir. I said, "There wasn't any pain." And Mrs Parker then shouted, "What do you know about pain?"

MRS PARKER Well?

THACKERAY Was he *very* ill? Pain? Was that the reason?

MRS PARKER Yes, Inspector. Too much pain. But he was so brave. He never allowed it to trouble him. Every day, he always went for a walk.

THACKERAY And you ended it for him?

MRS PARKER I had to. He couldn't continue. The pain was getting too much.

SILVER Couldn't the doctors help?

MRS PARKER Doctors! What can they do?

THACKERAY Ah! I understand now.

MRS PARKER Doctors are a waste of time. Oh, they helped at first. They gave him drugs. But the pain came back. So they gave him stronger drugs. It never stopped. Weeks. Months. Years.

THACKERAY It's stopped now, Mrs Parker.

MRS PARKER Yes. It has. I had to do it, Inspector. I had to kill him. You understand that, don't you?

THACKERAY Is that your coat on the door?

MRS PARKER Yes.

SILVER I'll bring it across, sir.

THACKERAY Thank you, Silver. You'll have to come with me, Mrs Parker. You know that, don't you?

MRS PARKER Yes.

THACKERAY We'll leave Sergeant Silver here. He'll look after things. I'll send some men along later.

SILVER Put this coat round you.

MRS PARKER Thank you.

THACKERAY You've got a beautiful garden here, you know. Beautiful. Look at those roses.

MRS PARKER They were his favourite flowers. He loved this garden. That's why we moved here…

THACKERAY Take my arm, Mrs Parker. That's better. It's a nice day. We'll walk down the hill to the police station. And you can tell me about him on the way.

The driver didn't stop

CHARACTERS

INSPECTOR THACKERAY
SERGEANT SILVER
JOHN PALMER
SYLVIA PALMER

Scene 1

(It is raining heavily. A strong wind is blowing. Inspector Thackeray and Sergeant Silver are standing at the door of a large house in the southern part of Manchester.)

THACKERAY What a night! How many more houses do we have to visit?

SILVER Well, we've been to ten now and there are four more on the list after this. And I've still not had my dinner.

THACKERAY Dinner will have to wait, Sergeant. We must finish these calls tonight.

SILVER *(Knocking on the door)* Come on. Open the door. We're getting wet out here. *(He knocks again, more loudly.)* They must be deaf if they can't hear that. *(They wait. The wind blows more loudly.)* There's nobody here.

THACKERAY Somebody must be here. There's a car parked in the road out there. Let's both try. *(They both knock very loudly.)* There – I can hear someone now.

(The door opens a little. John Palmer's head appears.)

JOHN All right, all right. Don't break the door down.

THACKERAY Are you Mr Palmer, sir? Mr John Palmer?

JOHN Yes, but do you know what time it is? Who are you, anyway?

THACKERAY Police, sir. Here's my card. Inspector Thackeray. This is Sergeant Silver.

JOHN Police! What's the problem?

SILVER Can we come in, Mr Palmer? It won't take long. We're calling at a number of houses in this part of town.

JOHN All right, then. But please don't upset my wife. She's not very strong. Nervous, you know.

THACKERAY We understand, Mr Palmer.

(They go inside. John Palmer closes the door.)

JOHN Please come this way. *(They go into the living-room.)* Two visitors for us, Sylvia.

SYLVIA *(Turning off the television)* Oh, that's nice. But you both look terribly wet. Why don't you come over to the fire and dry yourselves?

THACKERAY Thank you Mrs Palmer.

SYLVIA Er, have we met before?

THACKERAY No, we haven't. My name is Inspector Thackeray and this is Sergeant Silver.

SYLVIA Police!

SILVER That's right.

JOHN Here – give me your wet coat, Inspector.

THACKERAY Thank you.

SYLVIA That rain hasn't stopped since this morning.

JOHN Your coat, Sergeant?

SILVER Thanks very much.

JOHN I'll hang them on the door.

THACKERAY We're very sorry to call so late.

JOHN Look, this won't take long, will it, Inspector? My wife is rather tired this evening.

THACKERAY I hope not Mr Palmer. You see –

SYLVIA It's all right, John. Please, won't you both sit down?

THACKERAY Thank you. *(Looking at the fireplace)* You've been out in the rain too, Mrs Palmer.

SYLVIA Me? No. I haven't been out, have I, dear?

THACKERAY Those *are* your shoes, Mrs Palmer, aren't they?

SYLVIA Shoes?

THACKERAY Next to the fire there.

SYLVIA Oh yes, that's right.

SILVER They're drying, are they?

SYLVIA Yes, they were so wet.

JOHN It's terrible weather for March, isn't it?

THACKERAY So you did go out then?

SYLVIA Oh yes. At lunch. You're quite right. I forgot. I put them there when I came in. But I was only out for ten minutes.

JOHN Yes, you went out to buy some milk, didn't you?

SYLVIA Yes, that's right. At Robinson's.

JOHN But what's the matter, Inspector? Why all these questions?

THACKERAY Well, perhaps you can help us, sir.

JOHN Can we? What's the trouble?

THACKERAY Sergeant Silver, you tell them, will you?

SILVER Yes, sir. Well – it's just a few simple questions.

SYLVIA Yes?

SILVER We're looking for a car.

SYLVIA A car?

SILVER Yes. There's been an accident.

JOHN An accident? Where?

SILVER The accident was in –

THACKERAY Just a minute, Sergeant. Mrs Palmer, when did you go out for the milk?

JOHN It was one o'clock.

THACKERAY *Mrs* Palmer, please.

SYLVIA Yes, that's right. One o'clock.

THACKERAY You're certain about that?

SYLVIA Oh yes, I'm certain. Today is Wednesday.

SILVER Wednesday?

SYLVIA Yes. They close at a quarter past one on Wednesday afternoon.

THACKERAY Oh well. It wasn't you then.

JOHN What kind of accident was it?

THACKERAY A car accident. The driver didn't stop.

SILVER And he knocked down a child.

SYLVIA A bad accident?

THACKERAY A broken arm and a broken leg.

SYLVIA Poor little girl.

THACKERAY Yes. And only seven. The same age as mine.

JOHN But we didn't do it. You don't think that, do you?

SILVER We're just looking for answers, sir. Just a few facts.

JOHN What facts?

SILVER Well, the car. The child saw a black car. And your car…?

JOHN Yes, yes, we have a black car, Sergeant. But – er…

SILVER Yes, sir?

JOHN There must be hundreds of black cars in Britain. Thousands.

SYLVIA Why are you asking about ours?

THACKERAY Well, Mrs Palmer, the child also saw the car number. Well – part of it.

SILVER Yes, I made a note of it – 7 K.

THACKERAY Seven K, that's right. Just 7 K. Mr Palmer, what's your car number?

JOHN M447 KLN

THACKERAY M447 KLN. And do you drive, Mrs Palmer?

SYLVIA Yes, I do. But why?

THACKERAY The driver of the car was a woman.

JOHN Ah, so that's the trouble. Our car is black. It's got 7 K in the number. And my wife drives.

THACKERAY I've not finished yet, sir.

JOHN But it wasn't Sylvia at the accident. She hasn't been near Queen Street. We haven't been out this evening. You're just making trouble, Inspector.

SYLVIA It's all right, dear. The police have to ask these questions.

SILVER May we see your car, sir?

JOHN Which one?

SILVER You have two?

JOHN Yes. One's in the garage.

SILVER We'll just see the one with 7 K in the number.

SYLVIA That's the one in the road.

THACKERAY In the road? But that's a minute's walk from the house. Do you always park it so far away?

JOHN No. Only when it's very wet.

SYLVIA The path to the house is too soft for the car in wet weather.

SILVER That's true. We had to walk through that water on the path.

THE DRIVER DIDN'T STOP

THACKERAY Yes, you'll soon need a boat out there, not a car. Still, we must go, Sergeant. I do love these big country fires. But if I sit here much longer, I'll burn.

SYLVIA It *is* a good fire, isn't it? We like to be warm.

JOHN I'll get your coats.

THACKERAY And yours and your wife's too, sir.

JOHN But why?

THACKERAY Well, sir. One of you was the driver of that car in the accident.

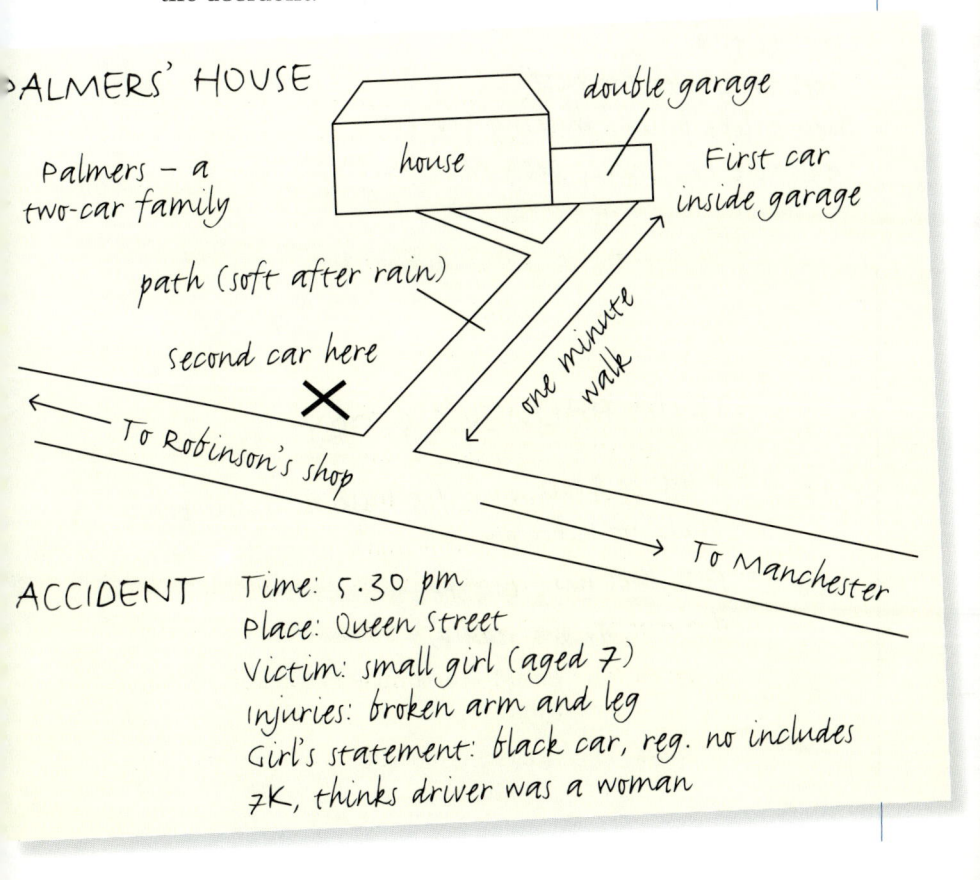

PALMERS' HOUSE

Palmers – a two-car family

house

double garage

First car inside garage

path (soft after rain)

second car here ✗

one minute walk

← To Robinson's shop

→ To Manchester

ACCIDENT Time: 5.30 pm
Place: Queen Street
Victim: small girl (aged 7)
Injuries: broken arm and leg
Girl's statement: black car, reg. no includes 7K, thinks driver was a woman

43

M447 KLN – POSSIBLE DRIVERS

Sylvia Palmer
Age – about 28
Quiet, polite (afraid?)
Feels sorry for girl in accident

John Palmer
Age – early thirties
Likes to talk
Tries to answer for wife
Doesn't like police "making trouble"
Says wife has "never been near Queen Street"

SYLVIA PALMER'S STORY

- went to Robinson's for milk at 1.00 pm
- back at 1.10 pm
- put shoes next to fire
- did not go out again

Scene 2

Inspector Thackeray explains

(Manchester Central Police Station. The office of Inspector Thackeray and Sergeant Silver.)

THACKERAY I'm sorry my office is so small. But I'm like you – I don't have many visitors. Just the sergeant here usually.

JOHN For the last time, Inspector. Neither Sylvia nor I went out this evening. How many times must I tell you?

SYLVIA Don't get angry, dear. It doesn't really help.

JOHN But all these 'facts'. They're just not true.

THACKERAY Well now, do you remember those shoes? The ones next to the fire?

SYLVIA Yes, of course I do. They were mine.

SILVER They were drying, you said. I wrote your words down.

SYLVIA Yes, that's right. They were.

THACKERAY Still drying? But you were home in the afternoon, weren't you?

JOHN From ten past one.

THACKERAY And that fire was very warm. Remember? I had to move.

SILVER But the shoes were still wet.

THACKERAY You were still drying them at seven o'clock this evening.

JOHN Oh, that was because –

THACKERAY Perhaps your wife will answer, Mr Palmer.

SYLVIA Well – I think – I put the shoes there just before you came.

THACKERAY Notebook, Sergeant?

SILVER You put them beside the fire at lunchtime, Mrs Palmer. Your own words: "I put them there when I came in."

SYLVIA I don't remember.

THACKERAY Read the part about the accident, Sergeant.

SILVER Er – yes. Mrs Palmer said, "A bad accident?"

JOHN Oh, really! What does that tell us?

THACKERAY Later than that, Silver.

SILVER Oh yes, sir. The Inspector here said, "A broken arm and a broken leg." And then Mrs Palmer said, "Poor little girl."

THACKERAY But I never said the child was a girl. Now, Mrs Palmer, why did you say, "Poor little girl"?

SYLVIA Well – because...

THACKERAY Perhaps because you were the driver of the car. Perhaps because you knocked the child down.

JOHN Inspector Thackeray...

THACKERAY Ah yes. Mr Palmer. How did you know the place of the accident?

JOHN I don't know the place.

THACKERAY Oh, but you did, Mr Palmer.

SILVER You said, "My wife hasn't been near Queen Street."

THACKERAY Queen Street, Mr Palmer? Now why did you say that? We never talked about Queen Street.

SYLVIA Oh stop it, stop it. It was me, Inspector. I did it. It wasn't John. He was at home.

THACKERAY Very well, Mrs Palmer. Are you ready to give us the facts now?

SYLVIA Yes, I am.

THACKERAY Good. I want the true story this time, Mrs Palmer. And I want it quickly. Open that notebook again, Sergeant. We've wasted enough time already today.

The game of chess

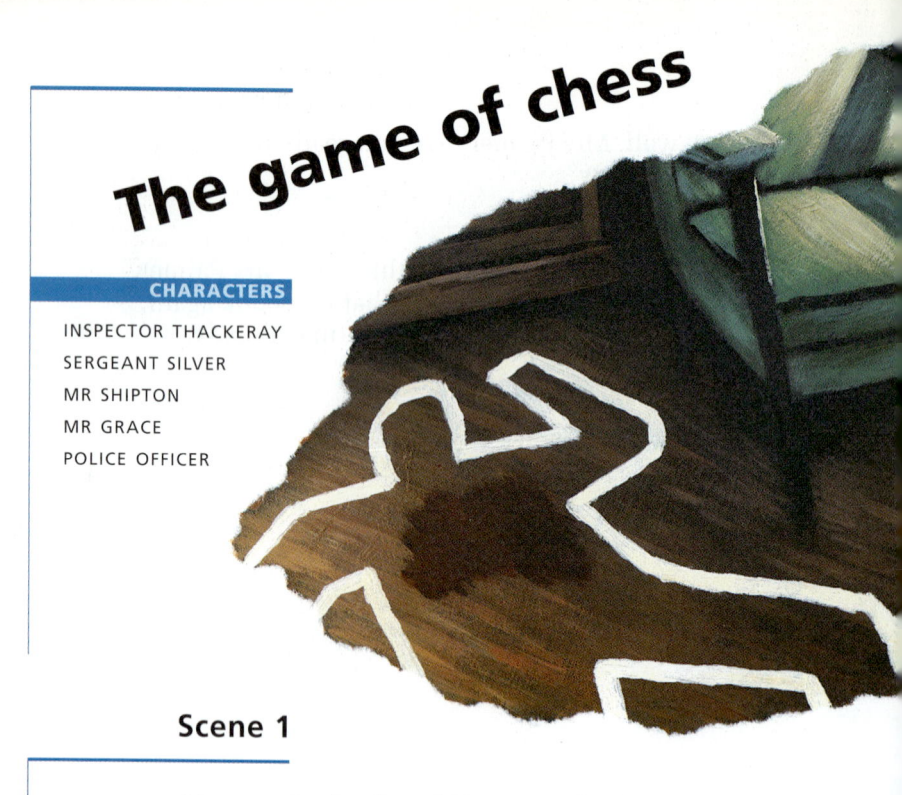

CHARACTERS

INSPECTOR THACKERAY
SERGEANT SILVER
MR SHIPTON
MR GRACE
POLICE OFFICER

Scene 1

(A room in the flat of Mr Peter Black, a rich businessman. Mr Shipton, his business partner, is sitting in a chair next to a large desk. He has a tired, sad look on his face. Inspector Thackeray and Sergeant Silver are looking at him.)

THACKERAY Well. Now the doctor has taken the body away – we can have a little talk, Mr Shipton.

SHIPTON Yes, of course. A terrible thing to happen. Terrible.

THACKERAY Sergeant Silver here will take notes. Mr Black owns this place, does he?

SHIPTON Yes, he does – he did. He's lived in this flat for many years.

SILVER Mr *Peter* Black, was it?

THE GAME OF CHESS

SHIPTON   That's right. Poor old Peter. We've been great friends for years.

THACKERAY   Now then. He died just here.

SHIPTON   Yes. On the floor, in front of us. With a knife in his back.

THACKERAY   He was in his pyjamas. Red pyjamas, and – er – some kind of dressing-gown.

SHIPTON   Brown.

THACKERAY   Oh?

SILVER   Was he wearing that earlier this evening, sir?

SHIPTON   Yes. Dressing-gown and pyjamas. He was certainly wearing them when I was here.

THACKERAY   All right. Now, what's in the room here? A bottle on the table. And two glasses.

SILVER   *(Writing)* A whisky bottle. Empty. Two glasses. Empty.

THACKERAY And a game of chess.

SILVER Yes, sir. They weren't playing long. They only made – oh – four moves.

THACKERAY Really? So you play chess, do you, Silver?

SILVER Yes, sir. It's my favourite game.

THACKERAY I see. Good… And then there's this diary.

SILVER One desk-diary. Are there any names on today's page, sir?

THACKERAY Good question, Sergeant. Now… Wednesday the 27th…

SHIPTON There are two names.

THACKERAY What's that?

SHIPTON There are two names on today's page. Mine is one of them.

THACKERAY Well, Mr Shipton, how do you know that?

SHIPTON I saw the diary, when I was talking to Mr Black this evening.

THACKERAY What time was that?

SHIPTON Oh – eight o'clock.

SILVER And what time did you leave, sir?

SHIPTON Nine o'clock. I heard the church clock, when I was walking down the street.

THACKERAY And where did you go then?

SHIPTON Home. I began some work. But I needed a few figures about the business. So I phoned Peter.

THACKERAY But Mr Black didn't answer.

SHIPTON No. I thought it was strange. So I phoned the porter. He came up here and had a look. Then he told me.

SILVER What?

SHIPTON Peter was on the floor. Dead. Murdered. With a knife in his back.

THACKERAY And so you phoned us?

SHIPTON Of course. I wanted to help.

THACKERAY And you did help, Mr Shipton, you did. Perhaps you can help us now, also.

SHIPTON Certainly. How?

THACKERAY We still need a few facts. Now, you arrived at eight, and left at nine. You played chess for an hour then?

SHIPTON Chess. No. We talked business. We were business partners. I haven't played chess since school. But Peter was very good.

THACKERAY So you didn't play this game here on the table?

SHIPTON Oh no.

THACKERAY How many drinks did you have, Mr Shipton?

SHIPTON Drinks?

THACKERAY How many whiskies?

SHIPTON None.

SILVER The bottle's here on the table, sir. And it's empty.

SHIPTON I've never seen it before. Peter and I came straight here from work. And we talked business.

THACKERAY Did you leave this room at any time?

SHIPTON No.

THACKERAY Did Mr Black?

SHIPTON No. We just sat here and talked.

THACKERAY What's the matter, Sergeant?

(Sergeant Silver is looking closely at the game of chess.)

SILVER Me?

THACKERAY I know that look. What's the trouble?

SILVER Well, sir. It's this game.

THACKERAY Well, don't stop there, lad – I don't understand chess.

SILVER Well – do *you* see the trouble, Mr Shipton?

SHIPTON No. I don't know much about the game.

SILVER Well – they just started this game. But the chessmen are on the wrong sides of the board.

THACKERAY In the wrong places?

SILVER Yes. Look here. This Black Queen is on a white square. It ought to be on a black square.

THACKERAY That's a real beginner's mistake, isn't it?

SILVER It certainly is. *(Pause)* Shall I phone Mr Grace, sir?

THACKERAY Who? Oh yes. Mr Grace. The second name in the diary. Yes, Sergeant. Do that, will you?

SILVER Right, sir. The number is in this diary here. *(He dials the number. The phone rings at the other end.)*

THACKERAY Can *I* have a look at that diary again, Silver? Thank you. Mm. This is interesting. Grace's name is on every Wednesday page. Every Wednesday at nine o'clock. *(He puts the diary on the table.)* Mr Shipton.

SHIPTON Yes?

THACKERAY Did Mr Black have a visitor when you were here?

SHIPTON No.

THACKERAY Did he get a telephone call?

SHIPTON No. Oh wait a minute. Yes, he did. Just one.

THACKERAY What was it about?

SHIPTON I don't know. I wasn't listening. And it was very short.

(There is a pause. The phone is still ringing.)

SILVER Still no answer, sir.

THACKERAY He's probably in bed.

(The phone stops ringing. A man's voice answers. The Inspector moves close to the phone and listens carefully.)

GRACE Hello?

SILVER Hello. May I speak to Mr Grace please?

GRACE Speaking.

SILVER Oh, good evening. My name is Sergeant Silver.

GRACE Yes?

SILVER I'm speaking from the home of Peter Black.

GRACE Oh? Are you the police?

SILVER Yes, sir. What time did you leave here this evening?

GRACE This evening? I wasn't with Mr Black this evening.

SILVER Your name's in his diary, sir.

GRACE Oh yes. But what's the matter?

SILVER I'm just trying to find some facts, sir. So you weren't here this evening at any time?

GRACE That's right. I had trouble with my car. I couldn't start it. I phoned Peter at ten to nine, and told him. I said I wasn't coming. Why don't you ask *him?*

SILVER Do you drink whisky, sir?

GRACE Well, yes. How did you know?

SILVER Mr Black has some here for you.

GRACE Ah yes. We always have a glass together on Wednesday. After our game of chess. But why are you phoning, Sergeant?

SILVER I'll be able to tell you later, sir. Goodnight. *(He puts the phone down.)* So, Mr Shipton. Mr Grace made that phone call to Mr Black this evening.

SHIPTON Did he? Why are you telling me? I don't know Mr Grace.

THACKERAY You don't?

SHIPTON No. I've only just heard of him from you.

THACKERAY *(Looking in a cupboard)* There's another empty bottle in the cupboard, Mr Shipton. Did Mr Black drink a lot?

SHIPTON Yes, he did.

THACKERAY Do you?

SHIPTON Never.

THACKERAY So you didn't have a drink tonight?

SHIPTON No, I didn't.

THACKERAY But he offered you one?

SHIPTON Of course. But when I refused, he put the bottle away.

THACKERAY Was he going to bed before you left?

SHIPTON To bed? No. I've told you. We were talking business. *(Pause)* But I think *I* ought to go to bed now, Inspector. I'm very tired. You must be, too.

THACKERAY It's been a long day.

SILVER Have you any ideas about the murderer, sir?

THACKERAY Not many. I'll think better tomorrow morning after a good night's sleep.

SILVER Tomorrow morning, sir! But we can finish this case tonight.

THACKERAY Can we?

SILVER Yes, sir. This murder is like the game of chess on the table here.

SHIPTON Like the game of chess? How?

SILVER It's full of mistakes. Beginner's mistakes.

THACKERAY Is it, Sergeant?

SILVER Yes, sir. I've counted four already.

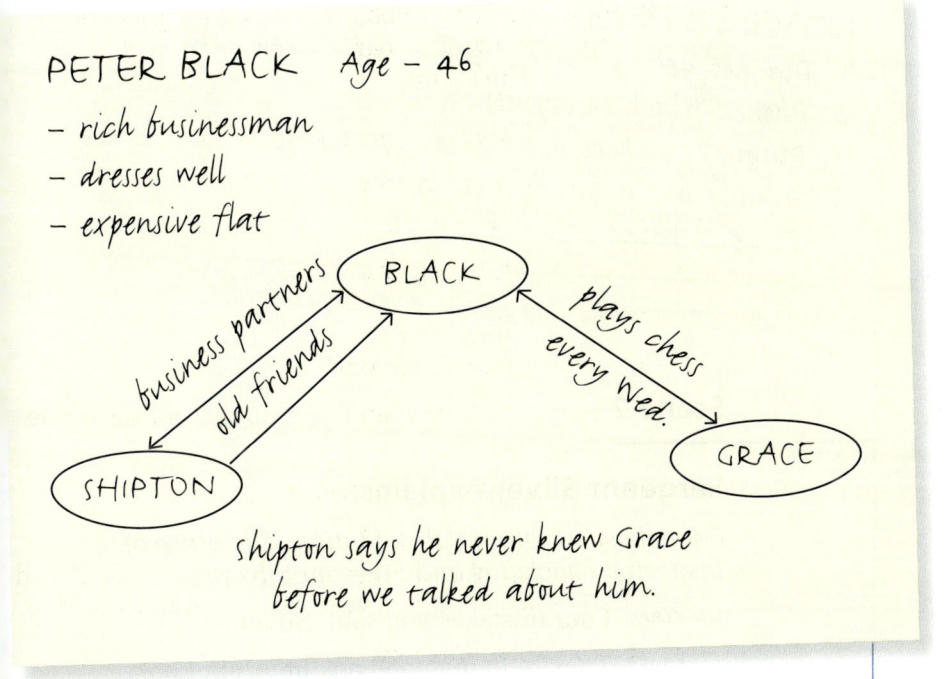

PETER BLACK   Age – 46
- rich businessman
- dresses well
- expensive flat

SHIPTON —business partners / old friends→ BLACK ←plays chess every Wed.— GRACE

Shipton says he never knew Grace before we talked about him.

SHIPTON'S STORY
1. Arrived at flat with Black at 8 pm
2. Talked business (saw two names in diary)
3. Did **not**
   - drink whisky (never does, refused when Black offered)
   - see bottle on table
   - play chess
   - remember name of caller on phone
   - leave room (nor did Black)
4. Left at 9 pm
5. Phoned Black later; porter reported death

GRACE'S STORY
1. Did not get to Black's flat, trouble with car
2. Phoned Black to explain
3. Plays chess there every Wed. (good player)
6. Usually has a whisky with game
7. Time of phone call – 8.50 pm

Scene 2

Sergeant Silver explains

(Manchester Central Police Station. The office of Inspector Thackeray and Sergeant Silver.)

THACKERAY Four mistakes you said, Silver.

SILVER They're in my notebook here, sir. Look.

THACKERAY Thank you. The light's not very good in this police station is it?

SILVER I'll put the second one on.

THACKERAY Yes. That's better. I'm sorry, lad. I'll never finish this now. You've written three, four, five pages! No. I've got a better idea. *(He picks up the phone and dials.)* Hello. Constable Brook? Thackeray here. Bring Mr Shipton in now. Oh, er, Brook, come back here again in, er ten minutes. That's right. Ten past one. *(He puts the phone down.)* I'm putting *you* in charge of this case now. Shipton's on his way here. You have ten minutes to question him. We can't keep him any longer. He's already started to get angry. This must be him now.

(The door opens. PC Brook shows Mr Shipton into the room and then goes out again.)

THACKERAY Ah. Mr Shipton. Do sit down.

SHIPTON Now look here, Thackeray. I'm going home. I've had enough of this. You can't keep me here any longer. It's one o'clock in the morning.

SILVER Please sit down, sir. I only want to ask a few simple questions, and then we can all go.

SHIPTON You're *not* keeping me here, then?

THACKERAY Of course not, sir. We don't think you are the murderer.

SILVER We just want to make certain of the facts.

SHIPTON All right then.

THACKERAY Sit down then, sir. That's better. Now Sergeant.

SILVER Well first, you saw your own name in Mr Black's diary – is that right?

SHIPTON Yes, that's right.

SILVER But you also said you didn't know Mr Grace.

SHIPTON I don't.

SILVER But his name was under yours, sir, in the diary.

SHIPTON Well, perhaps it was. But I didn't see it.

THACKERAY Didn't you? That's very strange.

SHIPTON No, I didn't.

SILVER All right. We'll talk about the whisky bottle for a moment.

SHIPTON The whisky bottle?

SILVER First, you said you didn't see it.

SHIPTON Did I?

SILVER Then you said Mr Black put it in the cupboard.

SHIPTON Well, that's true. I don't drink.

SILVER Then why did he *offer* you a drink, sir?

SHIPTON That's a strange question.

SILVER You never drink, do you?

SHIPTON That is correct.

THACKERAY Why didn't Mr Black know that?

SHIPTON He didn't know me very well, perhaps.

SILVER Shall I read your own words, sir? "We've been great friends for years," you said.

SHIPTON He made a mistake then. Perhaps he forgot. I don't know.

SILVER That chess game, sir. That was a mistake too, wasn't it?

SHIPTON A mistake? How?

THACKERAY   The Black Queen on a white square. You must remember that.

SILVER   You put it there, Mr Shipton, didn't you?

SHIPTON   I certainly did not.

SILVER   Then who did, sir?

SHIPTON   Well, they did. Black and Grace.

SILVER   But Grace didn't visit Black tonight.

SHIPTON   Didn't he? How do you know?

THACKERAY   And they're good players.

SILVER   Good players don't make mistakes like that.

SHIPTON   Oh, I don't know.

THACKERAY   And you're not a good player. You told us. You last played at school.

SILVER   You also said Mr Black didn't leave the room.

SHIPTON   Well, he didn't.

SILVER   But you arrived at the flat together.

SHIPTON   Yes. We came there straight from work.

SILVER   Then when did he put on his pyjamas?

SHIPTON   After I left, of course.

SILVER   But he was wearing pyjamas when you were with him.

SHIPTON   No he wasn't.

SILVER   But you said he was, sir. It's here in my notebook.

THACKERAY   Mr Shipton – you were wrong about the diary. You were wrong about the whisky bottle. You were wrong about the Black Queen. And now you're wrong about the pyjamas.

SILVER Did you kill him, Mr Shipton?

SHIPTON I did not. I've told you the true story.

SILVER I'll tell you the true story. First you heard Mr Grace's phone call. The phone was in the room. And you were sitting next to it. So you knew Grace wasn't coming.

SHIPTON No, no. You're wrong, Sergeant. Stop him, Inspector, or you'll be in trouble tomorrow. I'm an important man in this city, you know.

THACKERAY Continue, Silver.

SILVER Second. You were just leaving. You knew that Grace was not coming. Mr Black was tired. He wanted to go to bed. So he put on his pyjamas. Third – either you waited at the house, or you came back later. And fourth – you killed him.

SHIPTON You're making a very big mistake, young man. I'm an honest businessman, not a murderer.

SILVER Fifth, you put the chess-board and the bottle of whisky on the table. You made certain the diary was open at today's page. Grace's name was there. And beside it the word 'chess'. You wanted us to think that the murderer was Grace.

SHIPTON Inspector –

SILVER Sixth. You telephoned us later, from your house. You told us the porter's story. So we came to his flat.

SHIPTON That's not true. Peter was my friend.

THACKERAY He was also your business partner.

SILVER Mr Black is dead. Who gets the business now, Mr Shipton?

SHIPTON I do. But you can't say that I'm the murderer because of that.

(There is a knock at the door.)

THACKERAY Come in, Brook.

(Constable Brook enters.)

THACKERAY You're just in time, Constable. Take Mr Shipton to room twenty-five.

SHIPTON So you *are* going to keep me here.

CONSTABLE Come along, sir. There's a bed in that room. You can get some sleep.

SHIPTON You'll be sorry about this tomorrow, Thackeray. Just you wait.

CONSTABLE This way, sir.

(The two men go out.)

THACKERAY That was a good piece of detective work, Sergeant.

SILVER Thank you, sir.

THACKERAY Four questions and you caught him.

SILVER Yes. Checkmate in four moves. I like to play chess like that, too.

READING ACTIVITIES

Before reading

1 Inspector Thackeray is a detective. A police detective does one kind of police work; a police constable does another. Match the sentence beginnings under A with the endings under B to make true sentences about police work.

A	B
A detective	usually wears a uniform.
A constable	often has to control traffic.
	always wears plain clothes.
	often answers questions from people in the street.
	usually asks the questions in a murder case.

2 How can Inspector Thackeray find the criminals in these cases? Fill in the blanks to find out how he works.

First he _ _ _ _ _ _ _ carefully to each person's story.
Then he _ _ _ _ _ _ down the most important information.
He looks at the facts. He finds the facts which do _ _ _ agree.

3 Look at page 5. Who is talking to Inspector Thackeray? Why are they at the train station? What do you think has happened already?

While reading

1 Write down three questions to go with these answers about *The train robbers*.

Question	Answer
...............................?	Two million pounds.
...............................?	Three.
...............................?	In the guard's van.

2 As you read or listen to each play, you can look for the criminal, too. He or she always makes at least three mistakes. Can you find these? Work with the Inspector. Remember how he works.

3 In the third play, the Inspector and Sergeant Silver are looking for a hit-and-run driver. Make a list of the things they already know about
   a) the car.
   b) the driver.

   Who gave them this information? Look carefully at the detective's notes to find out.

4 In Scene 1 of *The game of chess*, how do you know that Mr Black's death wasn't an accident?

After reading

1 At the beginning of *Death at Hilltop Cottage*, Sergeant Silver thought Mr Parker's death was an accident. Why? Discuss this with others in your group. Do you agree with his views about crime in the countryside?

2 The crimes in three of these plays had a motive; the people who did them had a reason for doing the crime.

   Discuss the different motives in your group, and agree on the motive for each crime.

   The train robbers
   Death at Hilltop Cottage
   The game of chess

3 What makes the crime in *The driver didn't stop* different from the other three?

4 Time has passed, and these crimes have all been taken to a court of law. Imagine you are the judge of the court. What would you say about each of these crimes? Here is a suggestion to start you off.

   "This train _ _ _ _ _ _ _ was a very serious _ _ _ _ _. These men tried to rob the Bank of England of _ _ _ million pounds. I am sending them to prison for (?) years."

   Make similar statements to fit the crimes in *Death at Hilltop Cottage*, *The driver didn't stop* and *The game of chess*.

63

5 Part of a detective's job is to listen to people carefully and ask lots of questions. Look at these dialogues with a partner. They are about a bank robbery. Think of at least one suitable follow-on question the detective can ask each person, as shown in the example.

Example

CUSTOMER: I couldn't see his face, he had a stocking over his head.

DETECTIVE: Well, what clothes was he wearing? Did he say anything? What was his voice like?

WOMAN: The car drove off so fast, I couldn't see the driver.
DETECTIVE: ....?

SHOPKEEPER: I was just closing my shop, when he ran out of the bank.
DETECTIVE: ....?

BANK CLERK: I was so frightened, I gave him the money.
DETECTIVE: ....?

6 In *The train robbers*, the guard, Arthur Jones, gives Inspector Thackeray the information he needs. The three robbers are taking the money to the airport. They are planning to escape from the country.

Work in groups to write two short scenes. They will describe what happens next. Use this plan to help you.

Scene 1: The Inspector and Sergeant Silver drive to the airport. There isn't much time. They use the car radio to tell the police at the airport what's happening.

Scene 2: At the airport. The thieves are just checking in for a flight to another country. The two policemen stop them, ask questions and open their cases with the money. The men are arrested.

Act out your scenes to the others.